Doors & Windows

25

D1439416

Doors & Windows

100 PERIOD DETAILS

FROM THE ARCHIVES OF COUNTRY LIFE

MARY MIERS

AURUM PRESS

First published in Great Britain 2000 by Aurum Press Limited
25 Bedford Avenue, London WC1B 3AT

Text copyright © 2000 by Mary Miers
Photographs © by *Country Life* Picture Library

A catalogue record for this book is available from the British Library.

ISBN 1 85410 686 4
1 3 5 7 9 10 8 6 4 2
2000   2002   2004   2003   2001

Designed by James Campus
Series Editor: Michael Hall

Printed and bound in Singapore by CS Graphics

THE COUNTRY LIFE PICTURE LIBRARY

The *Country Life* Picture Library holds a complete set of prints made from its negatives.
The Library may be visited by appointment, and prints of any negatives it holds
can be supplied by post.
For further information, please contact the Librarian, Camilla Costello, at *Country Life*,
King's Reach Tower, Stamford Street, London SE1 9LS (*Tel:* 020 7261 6337).

Frontispiece: *Iford Manor, Wiltshire*.
Above: *Earlshall, Fife*.

THE remarkable archive held by *Country Life* contains over 130,000 black-and-white negatives dating back to 1897. For more than a century, these images have been central to the appeal of the magazine's weekly articles, playing an important role in shaping discerning taste and advancing knowledge and understanding of our Great Houses and smaller country seats. This unique visual record remains at the heart of *Country Life*'s longstanding reputation as 'keeper of the architectural conscience of the nation', words used by Lord Runciman as long ago as 1913.

This book illustrates, through the eyes of the *Country Life* photographers, the form and decoration of doors and windows through the centuries. It is intended to be both a gallery of beautiful photographs that can be dipped into at leisure, and a valuable source of reference for those seeking inspiration, as architects have always done, in the buildings of the past.

Country Life's formative years coincided with the domestic revival of the Arts and Crafts movement at the turn of the last century, when architects used vernacular detail to innovative effect, reviving casement windows and leaded lights, polygonal bay windows and oak-plank doors. From the *Country Life* perspective, this reinterpretation of the past was expressed most alluringly in the work of Sir Edwin Lutyens. A protégé of the magazine's founder, Edward Hudson, Lutyens received extensive coverage in *Country Life* and was himself influenced by what Christopher Hussey, a former architectural editor of the magazine, described as its 'sentimental quest for the romantic and picturesque'.

Many of the photographs included here date from those early decades of the last century, the heyday of the fine half-tone images which became the hallmark of *Country Life* and effectively transformed the taste of its readership through the series 'Country Homes and Gardens'. Early photographs, many of them of medieval manor houses taken by Charles Latham

Glenstal Castle, Co. Limerick.

(whom Hussey described as 'founder of the *Country Life* style'), established what he was to call a 'pictorial presentation of romantic atmosphere', transforming interiors into timeless and uncluttered works of art. They fostered a yearning for mellowed stone or half-timbered houses, reposing peacefully with the 'drowsy air of a vanished day' in some idealised English landscape.

From its early days, *Country Life* gave regular coverage to good contemporary houses in its series 'Lesser Country Houses of Today'. In the late 1920s, the articles became more informative and scholarly, and the magazine started seriously to record the great Classical houses of Britain, many of which were photographed by A. E. Henson, with interior views conveying key information about decoration, changing styles of curtain drapery, and furniture arrangement. During the 1930s, selected modern houses appeared, but not until the 1950s, when Mark Girouard joined the staff, did *Country Life* begin to record some of the great Victorian houses.

Charters, Berkshire (1938), and Gribloch, Stirlingshire (1938–39), mark the end of the chronological span represented by the black-and-white photographs reproduced in this book, but in order that some of the images might be arranged to convey relationships of style and mood in buildings of very different dates, they are not arranged in strict chronological order. Nor are churches included, since the core of the *Country Life* photographic archive is of domestic architecture.

In their functional, visual and symbolic roles, doors and windows provide the essential architectural language through which a building can be read. Any volume of Pevsner's *The Buildings of England* will reveal how important openings are to the understanding of a building, their position, size, materials and decoration providing important information about role and status, mode of construction and historical context. Often they provide the principal visual evidence by which a building can be dated.

The character of a building's main elevations owes much to the size, style and spacing of its openings and their proportion in relation to the overall scale. They establish its rhythm and may be employed for intentional repetitive or discordant effects, or to impose symmetrical order. A façade can be transformed by variations in the treatment of its openings – for instance, a change in glazing style or paint colour; even the temporary voids of windows left open can have an impact on the composition. The ratio of openings to wall surface has a marked effect on character and mood. At Hardwick Hall, Derbyshire, great glittering panels of Elizabethan glass appear to reduce the supporting stone structure to a thin skeleton, while in buildings with small windows sparingly disposed, it is the wall mass that is stressed, with the suggestion of solid impenetrability. The play of light upon a deeply recessed doorway, or a projecting porch, oriel or bay window, modulates the surface of a building, while its walls are articulated by varying the treatment of the openings to emphasise certain bays. Usually, the principal entrance bay receives particular attention, often by the raising of its doorpiece to incorporate a window with ornately carved surround, as at Blickling Hall, Norfolk. A strong vertical accent might be created by linking windows above and below with decoratively carved panels, while wide mullioned bays, lintels, sill bands and string courses emphasise horizontality. Today, influenced perhaps by the 'cult of the manor house' promoted by *Country Life* a century ago, we tend to favour fenestration that breaks up the surface with the subdivision of glazing bars or mullions and transoms over the somewhat blank stare of large plate-glass windows. Plate glass has a cold reflection which lacks the textural qualities of slightly wavy crown glass, and the variegated, glinting surfaces of leaded lights. Its principal appeal was, of course, the improved outlook it afforded, as it became increasingly desirable for houses to have rooms with a view.

Many of the photographs reproduced here depict details of Classical buildings, whose proportional relationship of pane, window opening, door and façade is governed by an overall unifying order. Their focal point is usually the main entrance, often part of an elaborate centrepiece – perhaps incorporating door and window within a giant order flanked by statues in niches, as at Castle Howard, Yorkshire, or aediculed in the Palladian manner. The hallmark of a Queen Anne or Georgian house is its regular pattern of windows, varied only in size and decoration to denote the hierarchy of different floors. Thus the *piano nobile* will have taller sash windows, perhaps with pediments and balconies, while those on other storeys may be corniced, or surrounded by simple moulded architraves. But Georgian windows can be deceptive about the function of the rooms they light. A study of

Arbury Hall, Warwickshire.

Robert Adam's plans reveals that the space behind his favoured motif of a Venetian window in the central bay was often subdivided into two small dressing rooms. More is revealed in the nineteenth century, when Gothic Revival architects sought to give honest expression to the form and function of their increasingly asymmetrical compositions, and the position and style of openings became more irregular. A staircase window might now be located, if necessary, beside the front door, and a feature made of it. In two of the 1930s houses illustrated here – Gribloch, Stirlingshire, and High and Over, Buckinghamshire – it has become a dominant feature of the design.

Those seeking a stylistic analysis of doors and windows, period by period, will find plenty of literature intended to advise the architect and inform the architectural historian. This ranges from manuals and pattern books by contemporary theorists to modern-day histories of style and decoration. Two important early publications were the seventeenth-century English translations of Serlio's *Book of Architecture* and Vitruvius's *Ten Books on Architecture*, whose Book IV provides detailed instructions for temple doorways and Doric or Ionic doors. The eighteenth century saw a flood of reference works, including Edward Hoppus's *The Gentleman's and Builder's Repository* (1737), books by Batty Langley, such as *The City and Country Builder's and Workman's Treasury of Designs* (1740), Isaac Ware's *A Complete Body of Architecture* (1756), and W. and J. Halfpenny's *The Modern Builders Assistant* (1757). Designs from these pattern books were widely adopted, and it was not uncommon for a window design to be borrowed for a doorway. Some publications were aimed at house owners, while others provided detailed instructions for carpenters and builders. James Gibbs's enormously influential *A Book of Architecture* (1728) was intended to be 'of use to such gentlemen as might be concerned in Building, especially in the remote parts of the country, where little or no assistance for Designs can be procured', but its designs could be executed by any workman 'who understands lines'. Today, handbooks and encyclopedias of architectural style and decoration abound. One example of a modern publication in the spirit of a Georgian pattern book, which

Sudbury Hall, Derbyshire.

includes a good section on doors and windows, is Robert Adam's *Classical Architecture, A Complete Handbook* (1990).

The range of doors and windows illustrated in this book reveals much about the technical developments of their day, and the fashion for and availability of different materials. Latticed windows had their origin in the medieval houses of a privileged few, whose rooms were lit by small panes supported by grilles or lead cames. (This style of fenestration was revived in the Regency period – notably for cottage orné Gothick glazing using cast iron – and again in the 1900s as the Neo-vernacular hallmark of many Arts and Crafts houses.) During the medieval period, any white glass of quality and all stained glass was imported from France, Flanders or Germany, hence its expense. Only in the sixteenth century did it reach a wider domestic market, and the wealthiest Elizabethans begin to flaunt their status by glazing as much of their façades as they dared, with great panels of leaded glass supported by stone or timber mullions and transoms. Some of the most beautiful windows surviving today date from the fifteenth and sixteenth centuries, their thick and uneven glass blending sensuously with the patina of weathered stone. At Little Moreton Hall, Cheshire, the lights are intricately patterned to a geometric design, while one of the most ravishing houses, Ockwells Manor in Berkshire, has diamond panes, some of stained glass, framed by elaborate timber tracery.

Until the advent of the counterbalanced sliding-sash window (an English transformation of a French invention), most domestic windows that opened were casements. Sash windows first began to appear in some of the grandest houses in the land in the 1670s and 1680s, and the fashion for this new style of sliding window spread quickly, encouraged by the necessity for a more vertical arrangement of fenestration as houses rose taller and were increasingly brick-built, as opposed to timber-framed. This coincided with the introduction of crown glass in around 1679, which increasingly became available in larger panes of cheaper and better-quality glass. At first, glazing bars (or astragals, as they are known in Scotland) were thick and unmoulded, acquiring

refined proportions and elegant mouldings in the eighteenth century as methods for producing larger panes of glass improved. The standard Georgian sash window, one of the most enduring features of British architecture, was generally six over six or eight over eight panes. As improved manufacturing techniques made cast iron more resilient, the nineteenth century saw a vogue for its use in windows, often painted to resemble wood.

Thorpe Hall, Northamptonshire.

The window tax of 1696–1851 had a significant effect, as did the heavy excise duty imposed on glass between 1746 and 1845, in controlling the fenestration of domestic buildings. It resulted in many blind openings, some of which were painted to appear real. The repeal of these taxes in the mid nineteenth century was timely, for sheet glass (a French invention) had become available in Britain from

Howth Castle, Co. Dublin.

with windows, the evolution of the door, whether mounted to its doorpost on hinges or pivots, sliding, or folding back in sections, is associated with technical developments and the availability of materials, as well as changing architectural style. Before the seventeenth century, most doors were of ledge and plank construction – typically, lengths of oak with supporting braces nailed across their backs. The panelled door, which became the standard type associated with Classical architecture, was common from the late seventeenth century. The arrangement and proportions of its panels – recessed, or raised and fielded – changed over the decades until, by the late

1832, and its manufacture over the following decades using different and cheaper processes allowed sash windows to become larger, with fewer panes of glass and glazing bars. The pioneering of hot rolled steel in the mid nineteenth century led to the spread of steel windows in the later Victorian and Edwardian periods; Crittal windows, named after their manufacturer, became a generic term. Many were designed to resemble the wrought-iron casements of the seventeenth century and fitted with leaded lights. The spread of reinforced-concrete and metal-framed buildings in the twentieth century gave rise to exciting possibilities in the use of glass as a non-weight-bearing wall material, able to span wide areas and continue around corners.

In most domestic buildings, particular attention is paid to the door as the focal point of the façade. As

Hill House, Dunbartonshire.

eighteenth century, six-panelled doors were the norm. Until about 1720, many doorcases featured decorative hoods on brackets, after which variations upon the Palladian style of door surround became the trademark of Georgian houses. The Gothic Revival saw the flowering of the lavishly decorated door and window surround. Its particularly popular motif of flanking colonettes with foliated capitals was to be adopted by countless suburban houses in years to come, as were the inset panels of decorative or stained glass associated with the Art Nouveau style around the turn of the twentieth century.

Internal doors were generally panelled to match the wall panelling until the seventeenth century, when they began to make more of an architectural statement. Increasingly they required the skills of a joiner rather than a carpenter, and often of other craftsmen fluent in carving, plasterwork, gilding, inlaying wood and decorative metalwork. A number of these photographs illustrate how the decoration of the door itself, and not only its architrave, might become integral to the overall decorative scheme of the room, as at Ham House, Surrey.

Many of the features and decorative details that have characterised doors and windows over the centuries had very practical origins. The porch, whose ancestor is the pronaos of a Greek temple, has the obvious function of protecting against the elements. Fanlights first appeared in around 1720 and reached their heyday half a century later, becoming more intricate with the introduction of metal bars in the 1780s. They were designed to light dark hallways, as well as to fill the rounded heads of door openings, ornamenting often plain Georgian façades with a cobweb of pretty glazing patterns. Shutters, origi-nally a house's only defence against the elements, became an important external protection for fragile early glass, as well as fulfilling other functions such as excluding draughts, controlling light, retaining heat and increasing security. Cornices and hood moulds were placed over windows and doors to throw off rainwater from the wall surface, with door hoods fulfilling a similar function. Windows were set back from the wall face to reduce the risk of spreading fire, an obligatory measure after the London Building Act of 1709.

The elaboration of a door with a porch or portico, sweeping stairway or triumphal arch gives special, sometimes ceremonial, significance to the threshold as a symbol of transition, leading from one state of being to the next. Throughout literature and the Bible, doors recur as potent metaphors, projecting 'images of hesitation, temptation, desire, security, welcome and respect', to quote from *The Poetics of Space* by Gaston Bachelard. With their furniture of lock and key, handle and hinge, letterbox and knocker, doors open to communicate and embrace, close to protect and hide.

The window – eye of the wind – transcends its practical functions of lighting, observation, ventilation and temperature control and becomes a gateway to the soul, a metaphor for vigilance and inner knowledge. But it is as orchestrator of light that the window features so alluringly in many of these images, preoccupying the photographer in his quest for clear, even tone and clarity of detail.

◁

Haddon Hall, Derbyshire.
Part of the great bay of
the oak-panelled Long
Gallery, superbly lit by
twelve-light mullioned and
transomed windows, which
were preserved and
releaded in the 1920s.
The Gallery was built by
Sir George Vernon in
around 1550 and
completed by Sir John
Manners in 1603.

▷

Haddon Hall, Derbyshire.
View of the chapel, which
dates back to 1427.
A cycle of late-medieval
painted decoration was
uncovered in the 1920s,
when the 9th Duke of
Rutland restored Haddon
from dereliction.

*Hardwick Hall,
Derbyshire. A bay in the
State Bedroom. Hardwick
was built by Bess of
Hardwick between 1591
and 1597 to the designs of
Robert Smythson.*

*Little Moreton Hall,
Cheshire. The geometric
glazing pattern of the
wainscotted hall bay is
similar to that at
Bramhall, nearby. The
house was built between
around 1440 and 1580.*

◁

Earlshall, Fife. A small leaded window with characteristic splayed jambs set into the thickness of the stair-tower wall. Robert Lorimer's repair and restoration of this sixteenth-century tower house dates from about 1891.

▷

Craigievar Castle, Aberdeenshire. One of the delights of the castle's romantic roof line is this ogee-roofed eyrie at the top of one of the spiral staircases that ascend to the rooftop viewing platform. It was transformed into a Scottish Renaissance château by William Forbes in around 1625.

△

*Little Moreton Hall, Cheshire. Looking through the outer doorway
of the gatehouse as it is approached across the moat.
The carved friezes, dating from the Tudor period, depict Italian
Renaissance motifs carried out in a provincial manner.*

◁

*Speke Hall, Lancashire. A view through the entrance porch,
whose arch is one of the few stone details in this half-timbered
Elizabethan and Jacobean mansion.*

OVERLEAF

*Little Moreton Hall, Cheshire. The spectacular gabled upper
storey of the bay windows, built, according to an inscription carved
in relief above, for William Moreton by Richard Dale in 1559.*

△

*Ockwells Manor, Berkshire. One of the hall windows, which depict
the armorials of Sir John Norreys and his friends. This mid-
fifteenth-century manor house has some of the best surviving
examples of domestic stained glass of the period.*

▷

*Ockwells Manor, Berkshire. Detail of the north-east gable bay
windows with cusped window frames and elaborate barge boarding,
all superbly carved in timber.*

◁

Wardes, Kent. Detail of the fourteenth-century hall house which forms the earliest part of the building. It was restored in around 1912 by Sir Louis Mallet.

▷

Rufford Old Hall, Lancashire. The heads of two doorways in the hall, enriched with low-relief carving of tracery and other Gothic motifs. Probably built by Thomas Hesketh, this is one of the finest surviving late-fifteenth-century halls.

◁

Boughton Malherbe, Kent.
Sir Edward Wotton's
Tudor bay windows.
The loftier upper tiers of
this two-storey bay or
oriel, made of locally
quarried stone, indicate the
position of the principal
living space.

▷

Cold Ashton Manor,
Gloucestershire. Detail of
window reveal in what
survives of the original
solar above the hall in this
smaller manor house of the
late sixteenth or early
seventeenth century,
renovated in the 1920s.

△

Four doors (clockwise from top left):
Cold Ashton, Gloucestershire; Hornby Castle, Lancashire;
Great Chalfield Manor, Wiltshire; Lulworth Castle, Dorset.

◁

Stokesay Castle, Shropshire. View of the gatehouse entrance, taken
from the courtyard, showing its elaborate timber-framed upper storey,
added in the sixteenth century. The moated manor house, fortified
by John of Ludlow, dates back to the late thirteenth century.

◁

*Forde Abbey, Dorset.
The entrance to Abbot
Charde's slender early-
sixteenth-century gate
tower. Founded on a
medieval monastery, the
house dates principally
from the sixteenth and
seventeenth centuries. Its
richly decorated oriel is
surmounted by panels
carved with Renaissance
motifs and Charde's
monogram.*

▷

*Clevedon Court,
Somerset. View of the
chapel at this manor house
of around 1320,
remodelled in 1570. It
seems remarkable that this
window tracery of
interlocking quatrefoils –
described by Pevsner as
'ogee reticulation' and an
extremely rare feature in
domestic buildings – is
contemporary with the
early-fourteenth-century
date of the chapel.*

◁

Avebury Manor, Wiltshire. This photo-graph of the library, taken in 1921, beautifully conveys the quality of light filtering through the weathered glass of the window, dating from 1601.

▷

Hardwick Hall, Derbyshire. The west front – 'more windows than wall' – seen through the entrance arch. Its great glazed grids of mullions and transoms, for which the mason John Rodes was paid 4d. a foot in 1590, heighten with each ascending storey and are arranged to provide rigid symmetry, sometimes disguising the true internal plan.

◁

Castle Drogo, Devon.
View of the great
staircase leading down to
the dining room. Built
between 1911 and 1930
by Sir Edwin Lutyens for
Julius Drewe, this granite
castle is at once
romantically medieval
and austerely modern.

▷

Fountains Hall,
Yorkshire. This narrow
porch contains the ascent
to the Jacobean Great
Hall, its four transverse
arches echoing the curve
of the oriel window, for
which they provide
support. The house was
built in around 1600 for
Sir Stephen Proctor.

◁

Lulworth Castle, Dorset.
The entrance to Lord
Bindon's hunting lodge,
1608–10, is a Classical
triumphal arch, possibly
Inigo Jones's earliest
work. The castle was
recently restored by
English Heritage, having
been gutted by fire in
1929.

▷

Canons Ashby,
Northamptonshire.
This doorway, which
opens on to the courtyard,
is believed to have origi-
nated in the Augustinian
priory which preceded this
Tudor manor house of the
Dryden family.

△

Blickling Hall, Norfolk. The entrance, viewed from inside the courtyard. The inner face of the archway is dated 1619.

◁

Blickling Hall, Norfolk. This heavily panelled oak door is dated 1620. Blickling was built between 1616 and 1628 for Sir Henry Hobart. The elaborate stone carving above the door depicts Hobart heraldry, along with the bulls of the Boleyn family, whose house formerly occupied this site.

◁

*Sparrowe's House,
Ipswich. Also known as
'The Ancient House', it
has an Elizabethan frame-
work of 1567. The present
appearance of its upper
storey, which swells into
elaborately pargetted
oriels of carved oak, dates
from around 1670. The
decorative panels represent
the continents.*

▷

*Hengrave Hall, Suffolk.
The gatehouse oriel is an
unrivalled example of
Tudor craftsmanship, for
which payment was made
to one John Sparke. One
of the richest and most
ornate of its kind, it is
roofed with half-cupolas
surmounted with crocketed
finials and borne upon
enriched corbel mouldings
supported by foreign
ornament. Hengrave was
built in 1525–38 for Sir
Thomas Kytson.*

◁

*Broughton Castle,
Oxfordshire. A late-
Elizabethan oak interior
porch, surmounted by
obelisk finials and a great
cartouche with coat of
arms, in what was
originally the dining room,
later the drawing room.*

▷

*Levens Hall, Westmorland
(now Cumbria).
The elaborately carved
doorway connecting two
drawing rooms at Levens,
remodelled in the late
sixteenth century for
Sir James Bellingham.
The door is treated in the
same manner as the
wainscotting, its doorcase
flanked by terms on
pedestals.*

*Ham House, Surrey.
This small and richly
treated miniature room or
'pickture closett' over the
west loggia is a little-
altered survival of around
1630. The florid enrich-
ment of its doors,
decorated by Italian
craftsmen in the same
manner as the dado, is
almost Baroque.*

▷

*Holland House, London.
Detail of the Gilt Room at
the house built for Sir
Walter Cope in 1606–07,
but destroyed in the
Second World War.
This room was among the
richest examples of
decorative taste to have
survived from the period
of Charles I, with
panelling probably painted
c.1625 for Henry Rich,
1st Earl of Holland.*

◁

Blickling Hall, Norfolk. One of the doorways which open at either end of the great stair landing, its florid decoration derived from Flemish designs painted by Vriedman de Vries. The interior was completed in 1628.

▷

Haddon Hall, Derbyshire. Oak doorway to the Long Gallery, completed in 1603, treated in the same manner as the silvery, walnut-grained dado panelling.

◁

*Tilley Manor House,
Somerset. The façade,
dated 1659, is enlivened
with heavy Baroque
ornament in a charmingly
idiosyncratic manner.
The door is flanked by
Ionic pilasters which
appear to be upside-down,
while the ground-floor
mullioned windows are
topped by outsized open-
scrolled pediments with
secondary detached
pediments above.*

▷

*Stanway House,
Gloucestershire. Looking
through the north arch-
way, c.1630, to the
forecourt, showing the
Elizabethan west front
with its oriel window and,
straight ahead, the inner
face of the gatehouse.*

◁

*Canons Ashby,
Northamptonshire. View
from the lower garden to
the principal part of the
original house which
incorporates the tower.
On the right is an
Elizabethan window, with
an earlier window above.
The segmental pedimented
doorcase and other
windows date from
Edward Dryden's
remodelling, c.1708–10.*

▷

*Tyttenhanger,
Hertfordshire. This
bracketed wooden door
hood to the south entrance
is an early example of its
type. The Queen Anne
brick house was built for
Sir Henry Blunt, c.1660.*

◁

*The 'Flying Cloud'.
The solid-oak 'shell
doorway' to the private
cabins of the 2nd Duke of
Westminster's yacht.
Detmar Blow was
commissioned to design the
living quarters, which
were fitted out in 1921
and reflected both ducal
grandeur and a taste for
the Arts and Crafts style.*

▷

*Tyttenhanger,
Hertfordshire. One of the
strangely mannered
timber doorways on the
stair landing, which
Pevsner described as
'quite crazy ... with
frames growing angular
excrescences halfway up
the sides'.*

◁

*Seaton Delaval,
Northumberland. The
Orangery by William
Etty at Vanbrugh's
Seaton Delavel, 1718–29,
is pierced by a rhythm of
round-arched windows
alternating with Doric
half-columns beneath a
row of singing and
dancing* putti.

▷

*Castle Howard,
Yorkshire. The monu-
mental centrepiece on the
north front of Vanbrugh's
Baroque palace, begun
in around 1700 for the
Earl of Carlisle.
A. E. Henson's photo-
graph of 1924 reflects the
sombre mood of this
elevation.*

△

*Trafalgar House, Wiltshire. One of the two unusual-looking
Venetian windows which grace the projecting half-octagon on each
of the two wings, added by John Wood of Bath in around 1766 to
Sir Peter Vandeput's house of 1733.*

▷

*Trafalgar House, Wiltshire. The principal room in each of the
later wings is lit by a Venetian window, on the inside of which are
cast-iron columns, with figures perched upon the cornice.*

△

Biddesden House, Wiltshire. View taken from the hall, with its round window arches and three oeils de boeuf *over the entrance. The house was built for General John Richmond Webb in 1711–12 and renovated by Bryan Guinness in the 1930s.*

◁

Biddesden House, Wiltshire. Trompe l'oeil *Regency figures painted by Roland Pym in the blind windows on the east front. Most of the ground- and first-floor windows have redbrick keystoned round arches.*

◁

*Blenheim Palace,
Oxfordshire. View of the
Bow Window Room in
the east wing, which was
designed by Vanbrugh
between 1708 and 1720.
The bow window is shown
here with its monumental
window draperies framed
by Grinling Gibbons's
Corinthian columns.*

▷

*Kelmarsh Hall,
Northamptonshire.
The saloon, redecorated
by Nancy Lancaster in
the 1930s with walls of
'cool olive grey' and silk
curtains to match.
The revival of American
Colonial taste influenced
her redecoration of this
house, built to the designs
of James Gibbs in
1728–32.*

*Houghton Hall, Norfolk.
The massive central
window of the saloon is
flanked by tables and pier
glasses designed by Kent,
all part of his original
ensemble for the
decoration of this room.
The carving is all of
mahogany, picked out
with gilt. The door faces
its mirror image at the
other end of the room.*

▷

*Houghton Hall, Norfolk.
The great saloon doorway
leading to the hall,
surrounded by wall
hangings of silk and wool-
cut velvet. The house was
built by Robert Walpole
between 1721 and 1735.*

◁

△

Rokeby Park, Yorkshire. This unusual Palladian house was built for Sir Thomas Robinson in 1725–30. This view shows two of the trio of arched windows on its east wing, their detail suggestive of William Kent.

▷

Wentworth Woodhouse, Yorkshire. View of the Great Marble Hall, whose six doors have pedimented wooden doorcases incorporating friezes of Siena scagliola. *This palace of Baroque and Palladian grandeur was built between around 1725 and 1768 for the 1st and 2nd Marquesses of Rockingham.*

△

Mereworth Castle, Kent. The Long Gallery, with its glorious coved ceiling painted by Sleter and sumptuously enriched doorcases with plasterwork by Bagutti, is one of the highlights of Mereworth, 1720–23, Colen Campbell's copy of Palladio's Villa Rotunda. The doors are unusual in being ten-panelled.

◁

Rokeby Park, Yorkshire. The doorway to the breakfast room, which adopts the Ionic order and has an entablature with just a simple roll moulding for its frieze, in order to accommodate the low-ceilinged room. The house was built in 1725–30.

◁

Inveraray Castle,
Argyllshire. The castle's
romantic Gothic Revival
exterior, begun in 1744 by
Roger Morris, disguises
the Classical elegance of
its interiors, created by
Robert Mylne in the
1780s using French
decorative painters. This
photograph captures the
light Parisian style of
Mylne's drawing room,
taken the year it was
converted to a dining
room, 1927.

▷

Honington Hall,
Warwickshire. Amorini
recline on the pediment
of Joseph Townshend's
magnificent door of
c.1740–50, probably
transferred to the Oak
Room from the saloon.
Like a temple front, it
stands slightly proud of
the panelling, c.1700.

◁

*Farnborough Hall,
Warwickshire. A corner
of the entrance hall,
which was designed along
with the dining room to
display Holbech's
collection of busts and
paintings by Panini and
Canaletto. This seven-
teenth-century house was
mostly rebuilt in the mid
eighteenth century for
William Holbech.*

▷

*Rousham, Oxfordshire.
This mahogany door in
the west wing belongs to
William Kent's library
addition of 1738–40.
Its later doorcase is by
Thomas Roberts of
Oxford, who redecorated
the room as a drawing
room in 1764, with
elaborate plasterwork in
the Rococo style.*

◁

*Rousham, Oxfordshire.
The library was
remodelled in the Rococo
style by Thomas Roberts
of Oxford in 1764, but
William Kent's bow
window of c.1740 survives
with its original glazing
pattern.*

▷

*Strawberry Hill,
Middlesex. A Gothick
doorcase in the gallery at
Strawberry Hill frames
the view into Robert
Adam's Round Drawing
Room, completed in 1770.*

OVERLEAF

*(left) Claydon House,
Buckinghamshire. Detail
of a doorway in the
Chinese Room, illus-
trating the prodigious skill
of the master carver Luke
Lightfoot, who worked
here between 1768 and
1771. The decoration of
the staircase and upper
rooms, as part of the
remodelling of 1754–82,
represents the apogee of
Rococo and Chinese taste
in Georgian England.*

*(right) Strawberry Hill,
Middlesex. Looking
through the drawing-room
doors into the ante-room
in the earlier part of
Horace Walpole's
picturesque 'Gothick
castle' on the banks of the
Thames, built between
1750 and 1790.*

△

Mottisfont Abbey, Hampshire. Rex Whistler's trompe l'oeil
*curtain arrangement, painted to resemble ermine and crimson velvet
as part of his theatrical Gothic redecoration of the drawing room.*

◁

*Mottisfont Abbey, Hampshire. View of the north end of the
drawing room in the west wing, redecorated by Rex Whistler in the
Rococo Gothic style, 1938–39. This extravaganza of painted
decoration is quite remarkable, for the whole thing is* trompe l'oeil.

Osterley Park, Middlesex. Detail of window and shutter in the Etruscan Room, showing leaf and stem enrichment running up the edge of the window frame. The decoration of the dado and shutters is almost identical to that of other rooms, such as the Tapestry Room, also decorated by Robert Adam, c.1773.

Nostell Priory, Yorkshire. A door in the boudoir (or small dining room) reflects the transitional style of this room in a house that combines the Palladian and Rococo. The door dates from the period of James Paine's work here, carried out c.1733–50, but its decoration in the Rococo style, with grisaille *cameos and pale-coloured arabesques, is by Zucchi, c.1770.*

◁

*Highclere Castle,
Hampshire. The music-
room door, designed to
match the Pompeian wall
decoration, which
incorporates some genuine
eighteenth-century
fragments. The interiors
were designed by the
architect Thomas Allom
for Sir Charles Barry's
remodelling of the 3rd
Earl of Carnarvon's
mansion between 1839
and 1842.*

▷

*Buckingham Palace,
London. The Chinese
Dining Room. The doors
and other fittings were
supplied for the Prince
Regent at the Royal
Pavilion, Brighton,
between 1815 and 1823.
In 1847, the room was
dismantled on the orders
of Queen Victoria and
its fittings taken to
Buckingham Palace.*

*Sledmere House,
Yorkshire. The entrance
to the most magnificent of
Georgian libraries, formed
by Sir Christopher Sykes,
1787–88, with internal
decoration by Joseph Rose.
Sledmere was restored by
W. H. Brierly after the
disastrous fire of 1911.*

*Southill Park,
Bedfordshire. Mahogany
double doors to the dining
room, belonging to the
most delicate period of
Henry Holland's internal
decoration at Southill,
dating from between 1795
and 1800.*

◁

Oxford Street, London.
Victorian shopfront, now
demolished.

▷

St James's, London.
Eighteenth-century
shopfront with Gothic
glazing in its round-
arched window heads.

◁

*Thatched cottage,
Badminton Village,
Gloucestershire.
Patterned glazing peeps
out from behind the fringe
of Thomas Wright's
cottage orné, c.1750,
with picturesque rustic
detailing.*

▷

*Wilsford Manor,
Wiltshire. The low
thatched nursery and
servants' wing of Detmar
Blow's Arts and Crafts
manor house for the
Tennant family,
1904–06, deliberately
evokes the West Country
vernacular.*

◁

20 St James's Square, London. The entrance to one of Robert Adam's finest surviving town houses in London's West End, begun in 1771 for Sir Watkin Williams-Wynn, restored in the late 1980s.

▷

Craycombe House, Worcestershire. The identity of the architect, who has captured the Adam style with fluent delicacy, is uncertain, though the house has been attributed to George Byfield. It was built for George Perrott, a merchant of the East India Company, in 1791.

◁

Sezincote, Gloucestershire.
The enormous central bay
windows in the Yellow
Drawing Room are shown
here with their original
elaborate draperies of
around 1825.

▷

Sezincote, Gloucestershire.
A view through one of the
delicately patterned
Mogul-style windows
towards the Orangery.
The house was built in
around 1805 by Sir
Charles Cockerell to the
designs of his brother, and
reflects the inspiration of
Daniell's Indian prints.

◁

Holmwood House, Glasgow. Alexander 'Greek' Thomson's ingenious treatment of fenestration is seen in the parlour of this remarkable villa, built 1857–58 for James Couper. Here, the lower panes move down-wards as well as up beneath a richly plastered ceiling that completes the semicircle formed by the bow window, making a full circle.

▷

Holmwood House, Glasgow. The studded dining-room door, decorated with applied paterae and roundels, is one of Thomson's most elaborate and unusual. A recent programme of restoration has uncovered the room's painted wall decoration.

◁

*Scarisbrick Hall,
Lancashire. One of the
highlights of Pugin's
convincing Gothic
remodelling, begun in
1837, is the elaborately
traceried fenestration of
the Great Hall, completed
in 1842.*

▷

*Penhryn Castle, Bangor.
The drawing-room door,
c.1830. Sir Thomas
Hopper's outstanding
remodelling of this old
Welsh castle in the Neo-
Norman style was carried
out between 1827 and
1846.*

△

Cardiff Castle, Glamorganshire. Detail of inlaid door.

▷

*Cardiff Castle, Glamorganshire. This ornately rich door of red
and gold, smothered in gilded ironwork, opens into the winter
smoking room in the clock tower. This formed part of the bachelor
apartments, William Burgess's later phase of work for the
3rd Marquess of Bute, 1868–73.*

OMNIA VINCIT AMOR ET NOS CEDAMVS AMORI

△

Door details (clockwise from top left):
8 Addison Road, London;
Madresfield Court, Worcestershire;
Dougarie Lodge, Argyllshire;
Ardkinglas, Argyllshire.

△

Hill House, Dunbartonshire. Window in the Art Nouveau villa,
which Charles Rennie Mackintosh designed for Walter Blackie
in 1902–04. The decorative treatment of its shutters reflects a taste
for the Japanese style and echoes that of the furniture
and fittings throughout the house, all of which were designed
by Mackintosh.

◁

*Great Dixter, Sussex.
View from the porch to
one of the hall bay
windows, added by Sir
Edwin Lutyens. This
fifteenth-century hall
house was remodelled and
enlarged by Lutyens for
the architectural historian
Nathaniel Lloyd in 1910.*

▷

*Encombe, Kent. View of
the principal bathroom,
c.1923, showing the open
large three-light window
with onyx columns. To
close the window, a heavy
barred frame slides into
the wall to the right.*

◁

Charters, Berkshire.
The ornamentation of
these inner entrance doors,
with their delicate
wrought-bronze grilles, has
a distinctively eighteenth-
century feel, in keeping
with the unexpected
country-house style that
characterises the interiors
of this striking Modern
Movement house of 1938.

▷

Encombe, Kent.
The moulded wooden front
door introduces a Baroque
element to the 'Hollywood
Spanish style' of this
seaside villa, built by Basil
Ionides for Ralph
Philipson in 1923.

◁

*Charters, Berkshire.
Seen from the garden, the
tall hall windows resemble
a great abstracted portico.
The all-concrete look of
the exterior is deceptive,
for it is in fact clad in
Portland stone.*

▷

*Baggy House, Devon.
The sculptural curve of
the staircase leads up
from the dimly lit hall to
the sunny upper spaces of
this clean-cut contem-
porary house perched
above the sea. It was built
for a London banker in
1996 to the designs of
Anthony Hudson.*

◁

High and Over,
Buckinghamshire.
The staircase window
takes the form of a three-
sided full-height glass
bay through which the
stair is seen ascending in
an elegant spiral.
This pioneering Y-plan
house was built in 1930
by Amyas Connell for
Professor Bernard
Ashmole.

▷

Gribloch, Stirlingshire.
The staircase sweeps up
across the soaring 'oriel'
of its central elliptical
hall. Gribloch was built
by Basil Spence in
1938–39.

LIST OF HOUSES

(in order of appearance)

These pictures from the *Country Life* Picture Library
were taken by staff photographers up until 1989,
including Charles Latham, A. E. Henson, Jonathan
Gibson and Alex Starkey. Pictures taken since 1989
include those by Mark Fiennes, Tim Imrie-Tate, Paul
Barker, June Buck and Clive Boursnell.

ACKNOWLEDGEMENTS

I would like to thank Michael Hall, Jeremy Musson,
Camilla Costello, Olive Waller, James Campus and
Clare Howell for their help with this book.